# REALISTIC DOUBLE FEET

## FOREWORD

REALISTIC DOUBLE FEET can be performed on a double bass drum set or a regular drum set with foot one playing ___ bass drum and foot two playing the hi-hat.

The book is grouped into twelve parts; each covering a specific rhythmic concept. At the end of each part there is an eight or twelve bar solo study. These studies combine all of the rhythms learned in the exercises and will give you the feel of playing the rhythms side by side.

### NOTATION KEY

Each exercise is notated as follows:
R.C. (H.H.) = Ride Cymbal (Hi-Hat)
S.D. = Snare Drum
F.1 (B.D.) = Main Bass Drum
F.2 (H.H. or B.D.2) = Hi-Hat or Bass Drum 2

### PRACTICE SUGGESTIONS

Play all exercises slowly, gradually increasing the tempo. To help develop a better "feel," practice all beats with records. Each exercise should be played at least eight times.

### ADDITIONAL PRACTICE SUGGESTIONS

1. Ride Cymbal: play quarter notes instead of eighth notes.
2. Foot Two: play quarter notes instead of eighth notes.
3. Foot Two: play on "and's" only instead of straight eighth notes.

---

### From the Publisher

Carmine Appice is a true drumming legend. Carmine was not only one of rock's first drum heroes, he was also an inspiration to me as a child. The moment I picked up Realistic Rock, I was hooked! (I subsequently collected all of his books, but Realistic Rock was my first Carmine drum book.)

I remember that it had a picture of Carmine's double-bass maple drumkit with a gong drum over the floor toms, double China cymbals upside down, electronic drums above the rack toms…I could go on and on. I was inspired, and I hadn't even opened the book yet! Once inside this treasure trove of rock rhythms and concepts, I found a virtually endless vocabulary available from which to draw new ideas and to perfect the important, solid playing that every drummer needs to know.

The benefit of working through Carmine's catalog is that it improves your playing quickly. You will save enormous amounts of time by practicing his exercises. This is the formula to fast-track your rock drumming prowess!

Modern Drummer is proud to present the entire Carmine Appice catalog, which to this day still inspires our playing! Enjoy, and we wish you the best always on your drumming journey.

**David Frangioni**
**CEO/Publisher of Modern Drummer Publications, Inc.**

---

Subscribe to *Modern Drummer*, the world's best drumming magazine, at:
www.moderndrummer.com/subscribe

For fun and educational videos, subscribe to the "Modern Drummer Official" YouTube channel.

---

Modern Drummer Publisher/CEO **David Frangioni**

Managing Director/SVP **David Hakim**

Cover drawing **Tony Laumer**

Cover design **Bill Conte**

---

Published by:
Modern Drummer Publications, Inc. • 315 Ridgedale Ave #478 • East Hanover, NJ 07936

# PART 1

## Eighth Notes with Foot 2

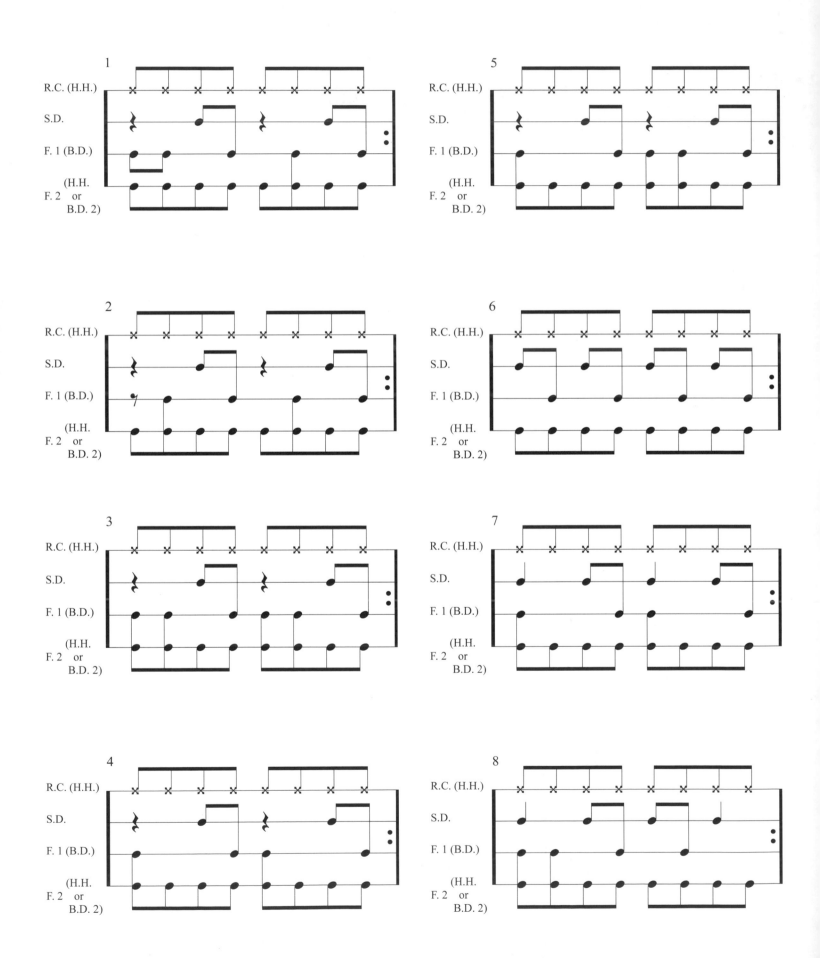

# Solo Study

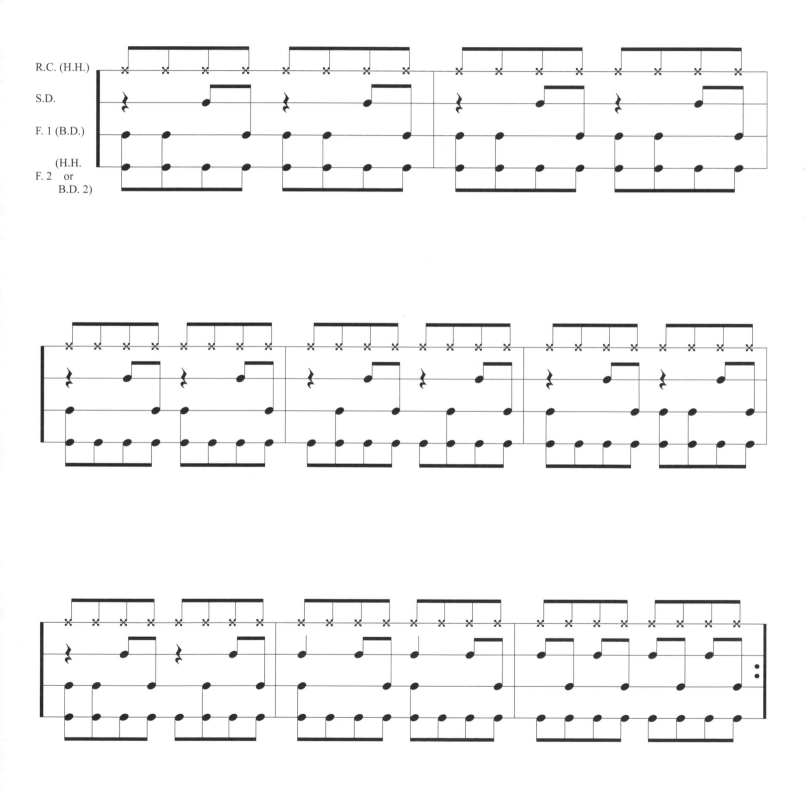

# PART 2

## Quarter notes on snare drum

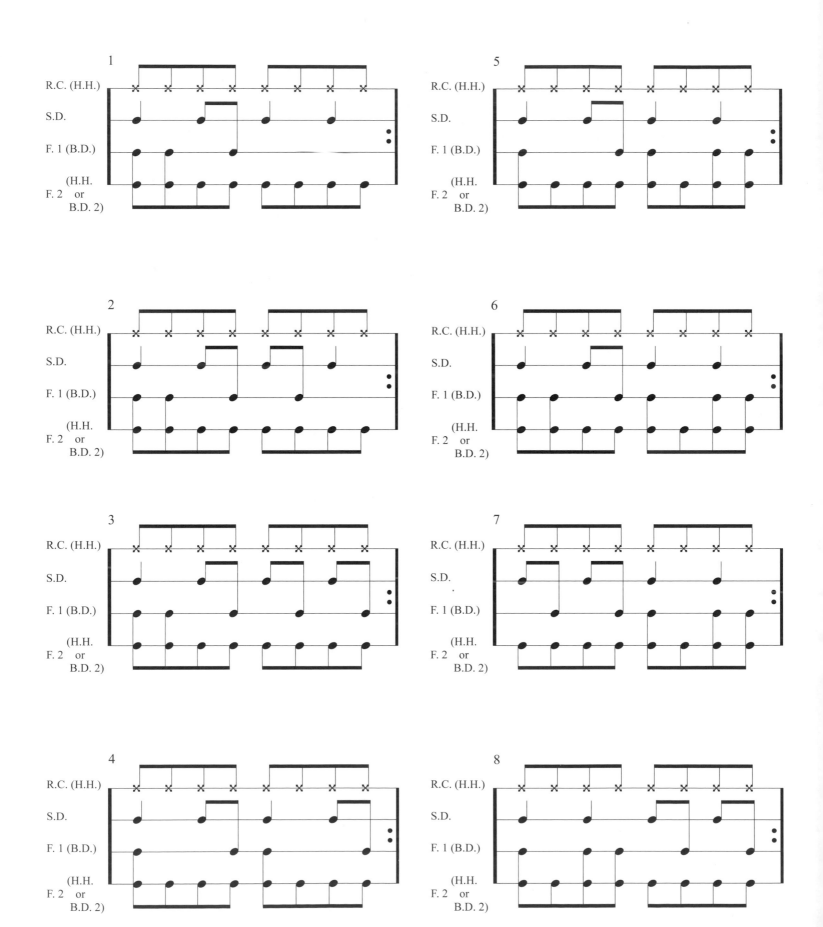

# Solo Study

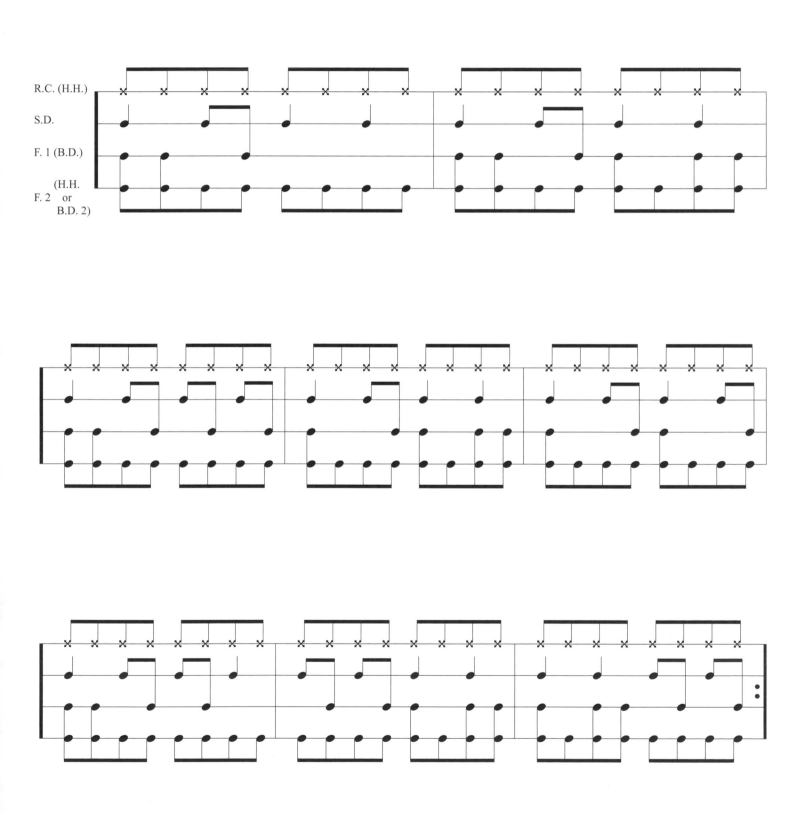

# PART 3

## Sixteenth note and dotted eighth and sixteenth combinations

There are four sixteenth notes to every beat. You should count 1 e & a, 2 e & a, etc. as you play them.

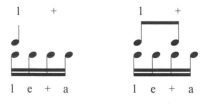

The dotted eighth note takes up three quarters of a beat. When it is combined with one sixteenth note, you get the following pattern:

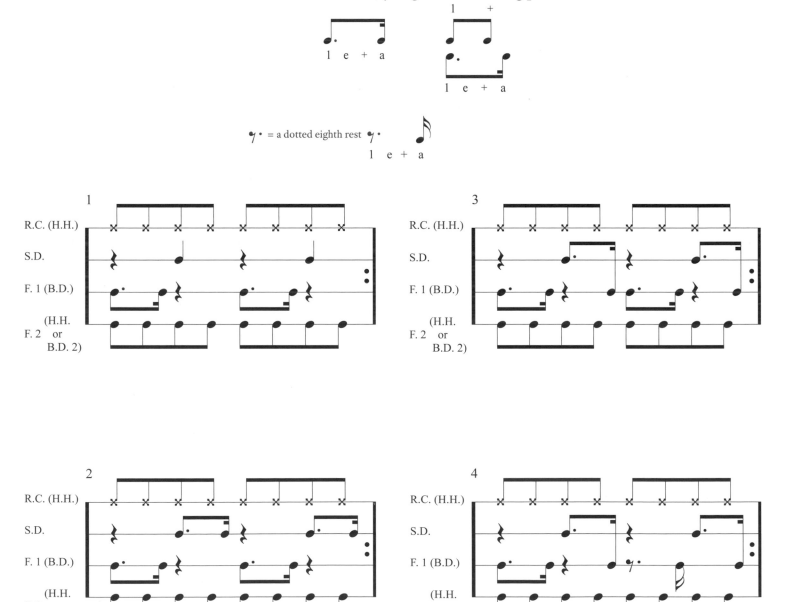

**5**

R.C. (H.H.)
S.D.
F. 1 (B.D.)
(H.H.
F. 2 or
B.D. 2)

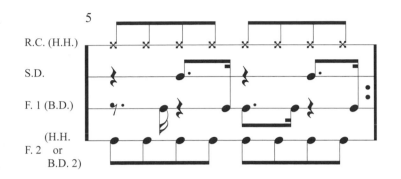

**9**

R.C. (H.H.)
S.D.
F. 1 (B.D.)
(H.H.
F. 2 or
B.D. 2)

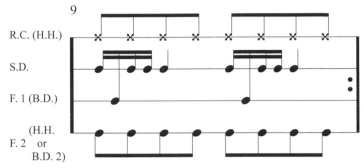

**6**

R.C. (H.H.)
S.D.
F. 1 (B.D.)
(H.H.
F. 2 or
B.D. 2)

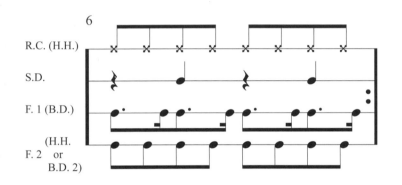

**10**

R.C. (H.H.)
S.D.
F. 1 (B.D.)
(H.H.
F. 2 or
B.D. 2)

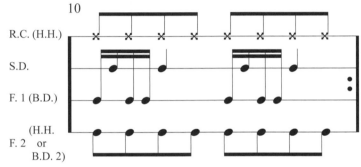

**7**

R.C. (H.H.)
S.D.
F. 1 (B.D.)
(H.H.
F. 2 or
B.D. 2)

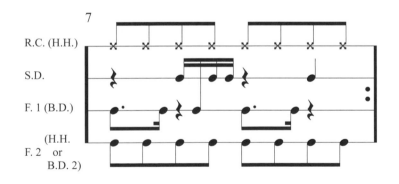

**11**

R.C. (H.H.)
S.D.
F. 1 (B.D.)
(H.H.
F. 2 or
B.D. 2)

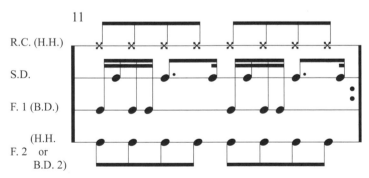

**8**

R.C. (H.H.)
S.D.
F. 1 (B.D.)
(H.H.
F. 2 or
B.D. 2)

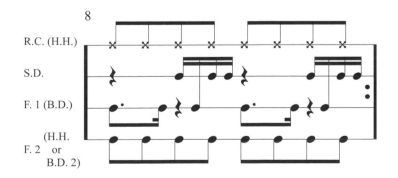

**12**

R.C. (H.H.)
S.D.
F. 1 (B.D.)
(H.H.
F. 2 or
B.D. 2)

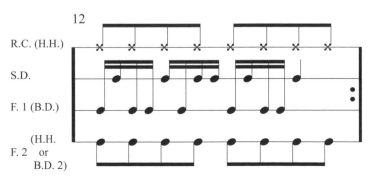

# Solo Study

R.C. (H.H.)
S.D.
F. 1 (B.D.)
(H.H.
F. 2   or
B.D. 2)

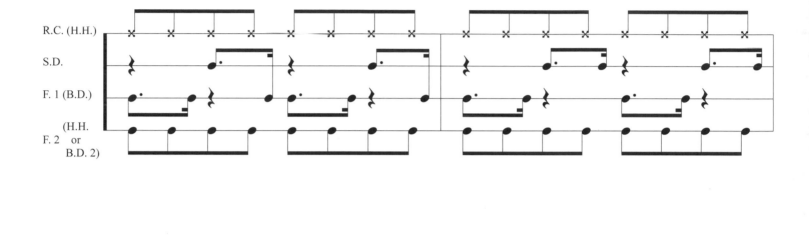

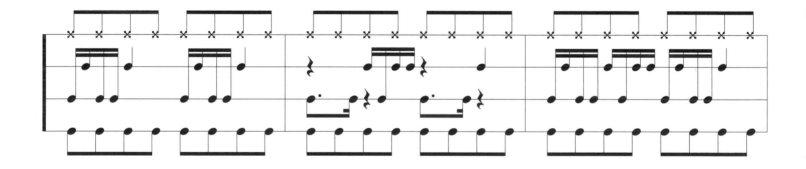

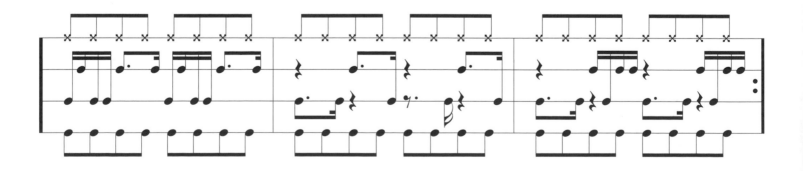

# PART 4

## Sixteenth variations

Sixteenth notes can be used in many different patterns by combining them with eighth notes and sixteenth rests (𝄾):

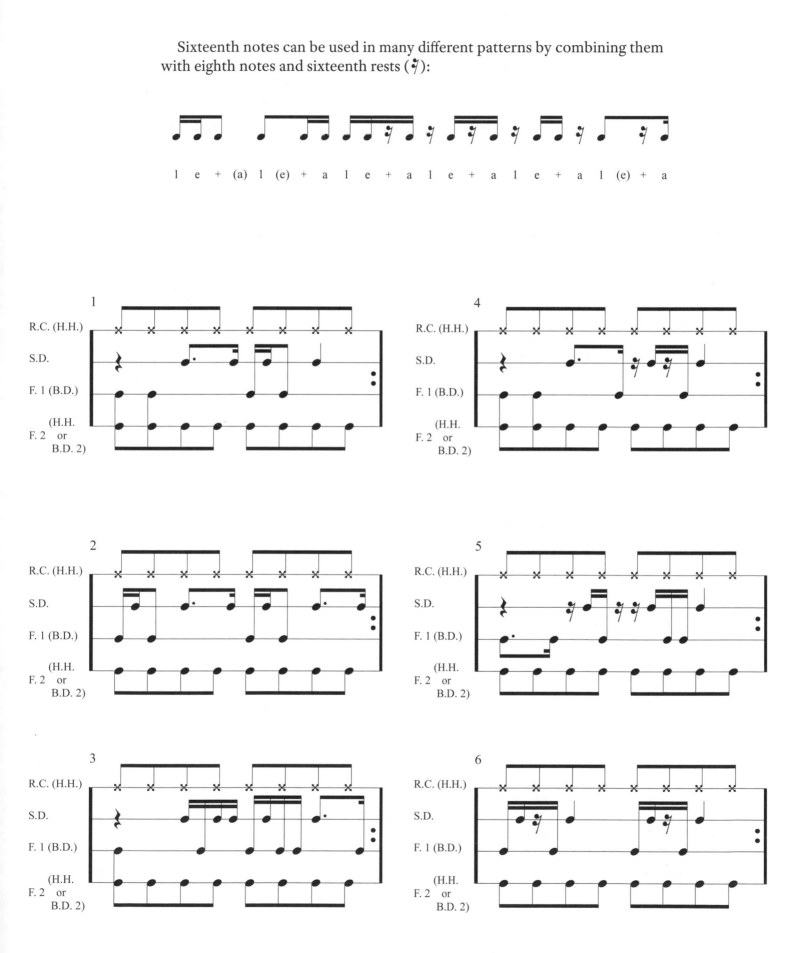

10

**7**

R.C. (H.H.)
S.D.
F. 1 (B.D.)
(H.H.
F. 2  or
B.D. 2)

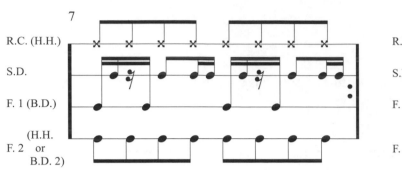

**8**

R.C. (H.H.)
S.D.
F. 1 (B.D.)
(H.H.
F. 2  or
B.D. 2)

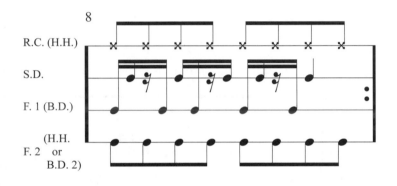

**9**

R.C. (H.H.)
S.D.
F. 1 (B.D.)
(H.H.
F. 2  or
B.D. 2)

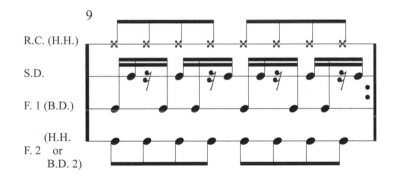

**10**

R.C. (H.H.)
S.D.
F. 1 (B.D.)
(H.H.
F. 2  or
B.D. 2)

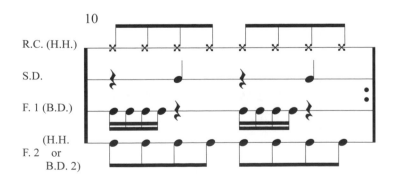

**11**

R.C. (H.H.)
S.D.
F. 1 (B.D.)
(H.H.
F. 2  or
B.D. 2)

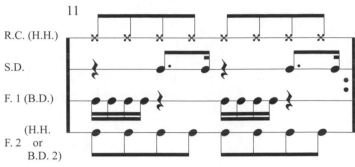

**12**

R.C. (H.H.)
S.D.
F. 1 (B.D.)
(H.H.
F. 2  or
B.D. 2)

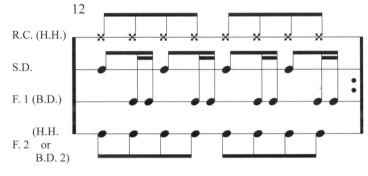

**13**

R.C. (H.H.)
S.D.
F. 1 (B.D.)
(H.H.
F. 2  or
B.D. 2)

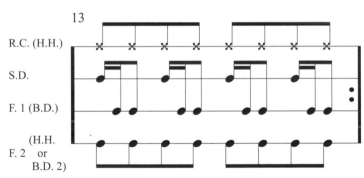

**14**

R.C. (H.H.)
S.D.
F. 1 (B.D.)
(H.H.
F. 2  or
B.D. 2)

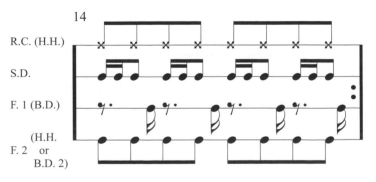

# Solo Study

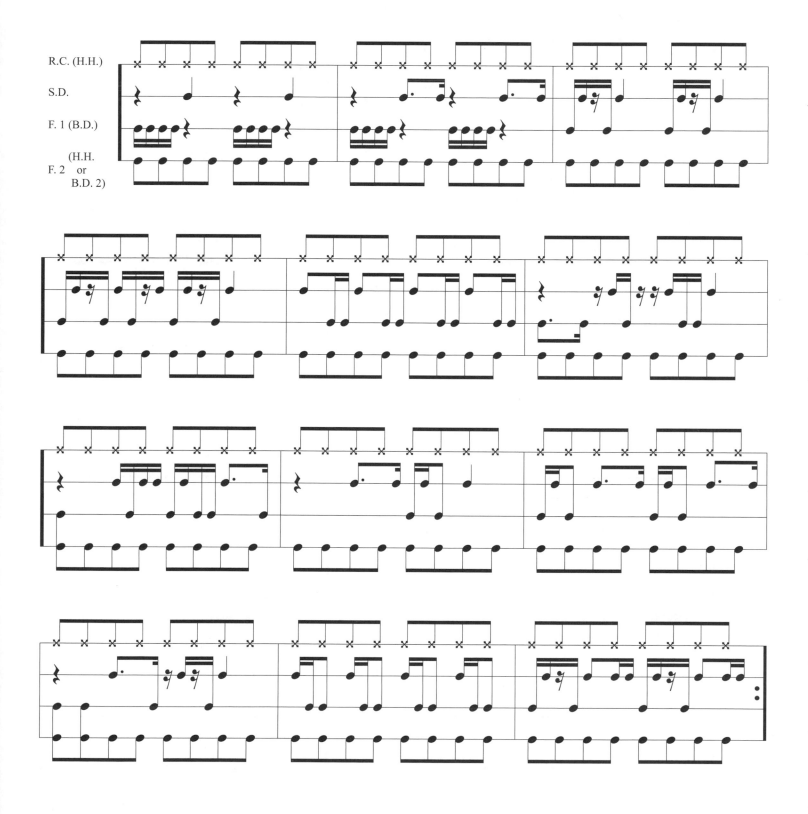

# PART 5

## Sixteenth variations between feet

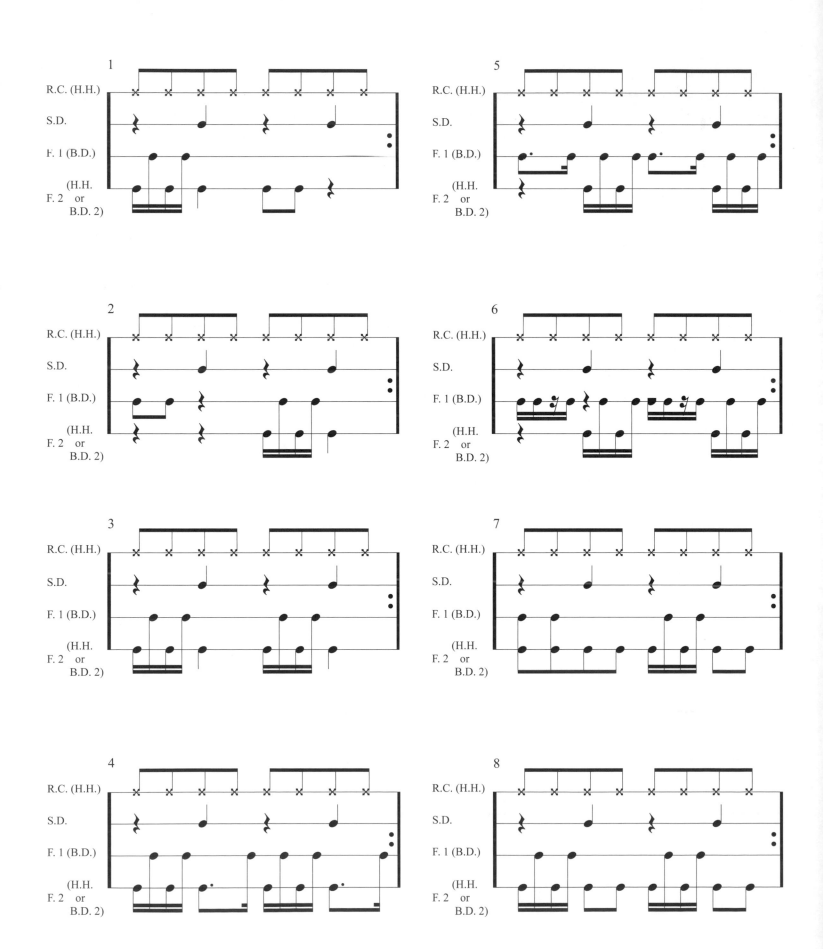

9

R.C. (H.H.)
S.D.
F. 1 (B.D.)
(H.H.
F. 2  or
B.D. 2)

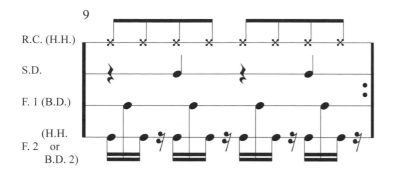

13

R.C. (H.H.)
S.D.
F. 1 (B.D.)
(H.H.
F. 2  or
B.D. 2)

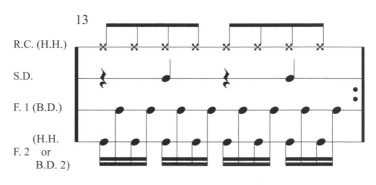

10

R.C. (H.H.)
S.D.
F. 1 (B.D.)
(H.H.
F. 2  or
B.D. 2)

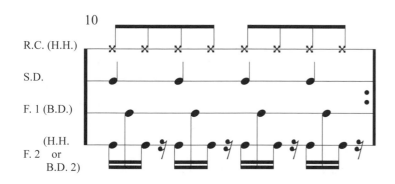

14

R.C. (H.H.)
S.D.
F. 1 (B.D.)
(H.H.
F. 2  or
B.D. 2)

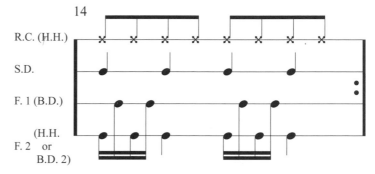

11

R.C. (H.H.)
S.D.
F. 1 (B.D.)
(H.H.
F. 2  or
B.D. 2)

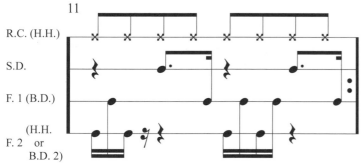

15

R.C. (H.H.)
S.D.
F. 1 (B.D.)
(H.H.
F. 2  or
B.D. 2)

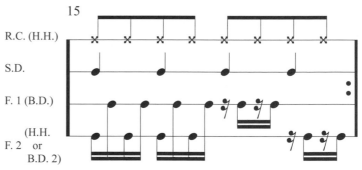

12

R.C. (H.H.)
S.D.
F. 1 (B.D.)
(H.H.
F. 2  or
B.D. 2)

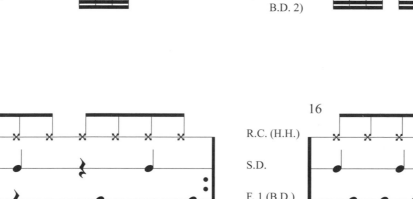

16

R.C. (H.H.)
S.D.
F. 1 (B.D.)
(H.H.
F. 2  or
B.D. 2)

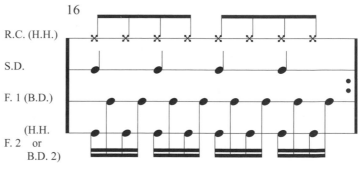

# Solo Study

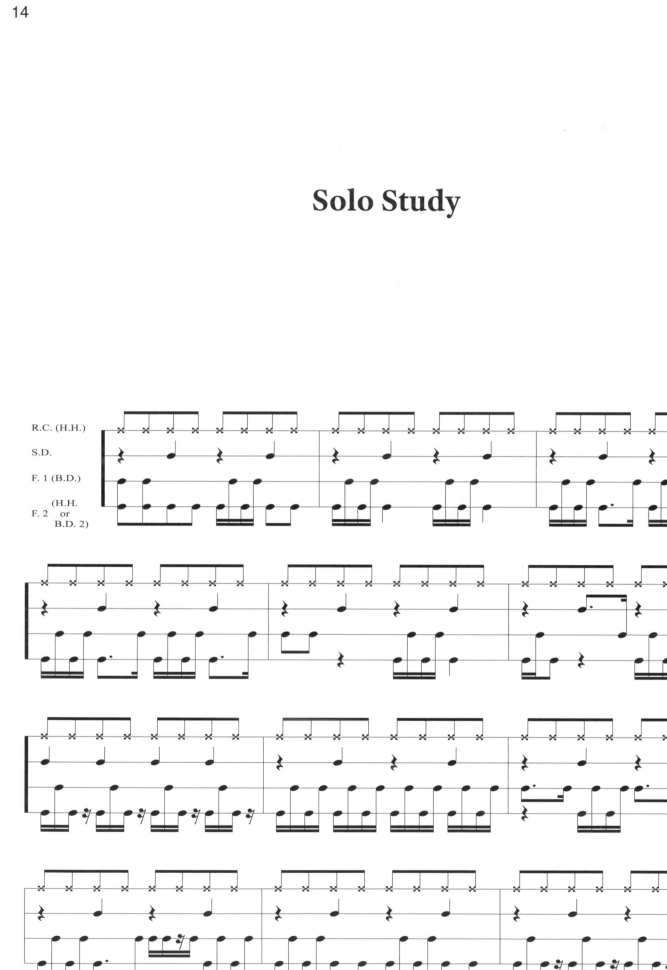

# PART 6

## Sixteenth triplets with Feet

Sixteenth notes can be used in triplet form. When you play sixteenth triplets you play six notes for every beat.

You will sometimes find a sixteenth rest substituted for the first note of the triplet. When this happens, the triplet fits between the eighth notes which are being played by the cymbal.

Figure the measures out slowly. Check out the relationships between the notes on all the lines.

1

R.C. (H.H.)

S.D.

F. 1 (B.D.)

(H.H.
F. 2   or
    B.D. 2)

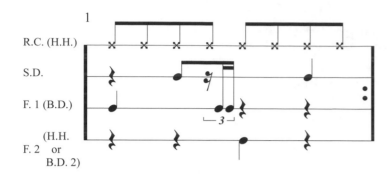

5

R.C. (H.H.)

S.D.

F. 1 (B.D.)

(H.H.
F. 2   or
    B.D. 2)

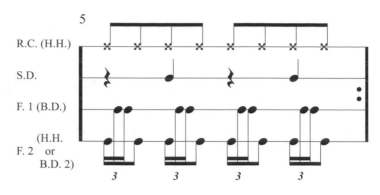

2

R.C. (H.H.)

S.D.

F. 1 (B.D.)

(H.H.
F. 2   or
    B.D. 2)

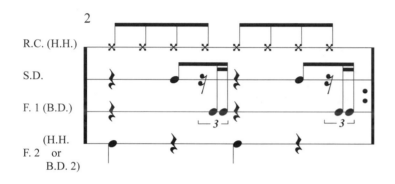

6

R.C. (H.H.)

S.D.

F. 1 (B.D.)

(H.H.
F. 2   or
    B.D. 2)

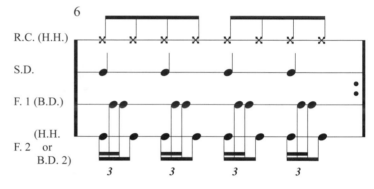

3

R.C. (H.H.)

S.D.

F. 1 (B.D.)

(H.H.
F. 2   or
    B.D. 2)

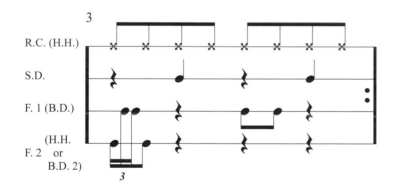

7

R.C. (H.H.)

S.D.

F. 1 (B.D.)

(H.H.
F. 2   or
    B.D. 2)

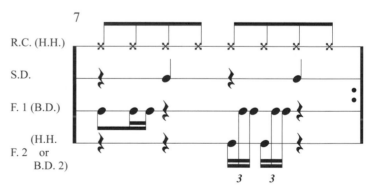

4

R.C. (H.H.)

S.D.

F. 1 (B.D.)

(H.H.
F. 2   or
    B.D. 2)

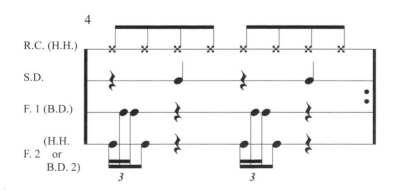

8

R.C. (H.H.)

S.D.

F. 1 (B.D.)

(H.H.
F. 2   or
    B.D. 2)

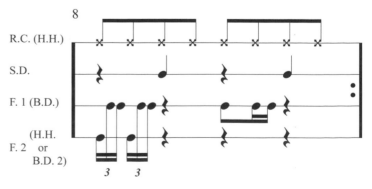

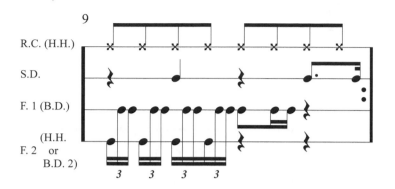

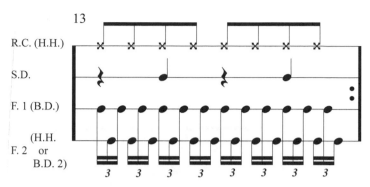

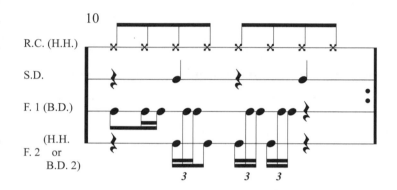

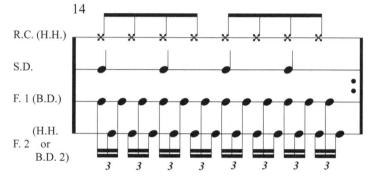

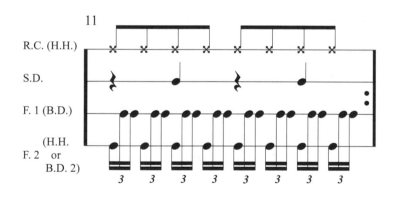

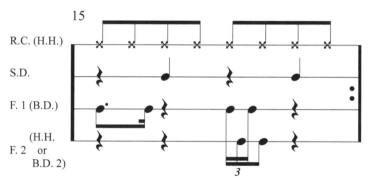

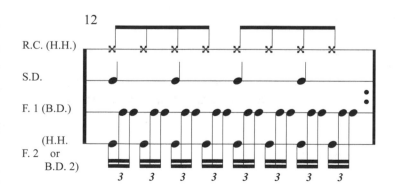

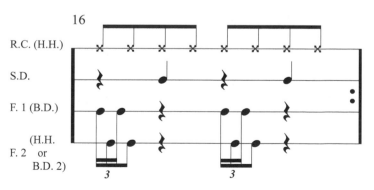

# Solo Study

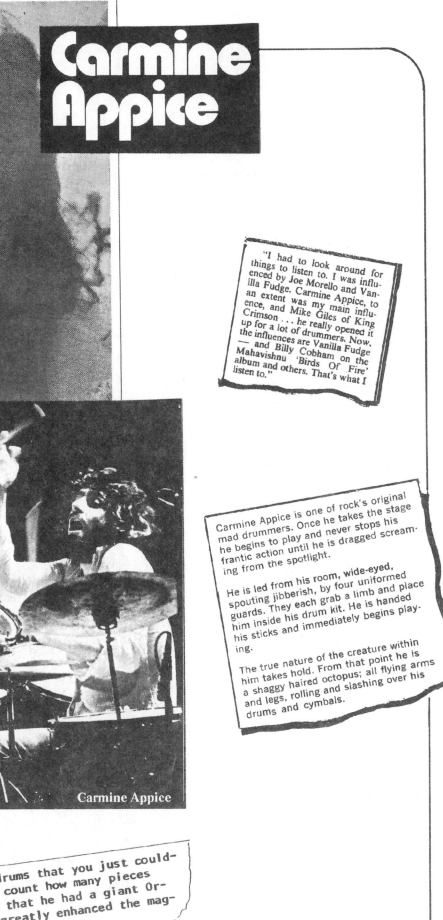

# Carmine Appice

"I had to look around for things to listen to. I was influenced by Joe Morello and Vanilla Fudge. Carmine Appice, to an extent was my main influence, and Mike Giles of King Crimson . . . he really opened it up for a lot of drummers. Now, the influences are Vanilla Fudge — and Billy Cobham on the Mahavishnu 'Birds Of Fire' album and others. That's what I listen to."

Carmine Appice is one of rock's original mad drummers. Once he takes the stage he begins to play and never stops his frantic action until he is dragged screaming from the spotlight.

He is led from his room, wide-eyed, spouting jibberish, by four uniformed guards. They each grab a limb and place him inside his drum kit. He is handed his sticks and immediately begins playing.

The true nature of the creature within him takes hold. From that point he is a shaggy haired octopus; all flying arms and legs, rolling and slashing over his drums and cymbals.

**Carmine Appice**

Carmine Appice had a set of drums that you just couldn't miss. I didn't even try to count how many pieces there were, but I might mention that he had a giant Oriental-type cymbal/gong, which greatly enhanced the magical feeling.

To remove poster:
Turn page, open staples and remove poster. Resecure book pages by pressing staples down.

# CARMINE APPICE

**SPEED PRODUCTION**

in association with

**INTER SOUND**

present exclusively in concert

Jeff **BECK**    Tim **BOGERT**    Carmine **APPICE**

ex VANILLA FUDGE

&

ex CACTUS

BOGERT & APPICE

& „Buffy" and his Guitar
Mittwoch 13. Juni 73   20h 15

# VOLKSHAUS ZÜRICH

Einziges Konzert in der Schweiz !

### The trio of all time !

überzeugendstes und packendstes was

ROCK MUSIC has spawned many three pieces in its time, names come to mind like Cream, Jimi Hendrix Experience and Taste, but recently I saw the rock trio to end all rock trios, Beck, Bogert and Appice.

Both Carmine Appice and Tim Bogert have „paid their dues" in Vanilla Fudge and Cactus and have through the years developed into one of the finest rhythm sections existent, while retaining their own individual techniques on their respective instruments.

At Crystal Palace Jeff Beck proved beyond doubt why he's rated as highly as he is, and truly gave a lesson on how to play the guitar.

For me Beck, Bogert and Appice stole the show and gave me one of the best performances I have ever seen. — **Gordon Irwin**, **Newtownabbey**, **Co. Antrim, Northern Ireland.**

Appice has been a legendary powerhouse drummer since his days with Vanilla Fudge. But until he started to work with Jeff he had not been seen much in England.

He is credited with being an influence on another great drummer, John Bonham, and undoubtedly his formidable technique and feel for rock, make him a formidable percussive force.

He has tremendous positive strength which combines a slickness not usually evident in such heavy playing. Hi-hats bark, tom-toms and bass drums rumble and his snare drum rolls are like a rain of fire. What was Carmine's background, and whence came that battering attack?

■ Jeff Beck — he's a monster. Wizard of the guitar, star of Beck, Bogert and Appice and temperamental genius, born of the British rock revolution. Carmine, Tim and Jeff stunned even their fans with a brilliant performance at the MM's Crystal Palace concert. Now they are busy recording a new album in London. MM's Chris Welch probes BB&A in action and wonders if rock music will ever be the same.

# PART 7

## Sixteenth triplets with hands and feet

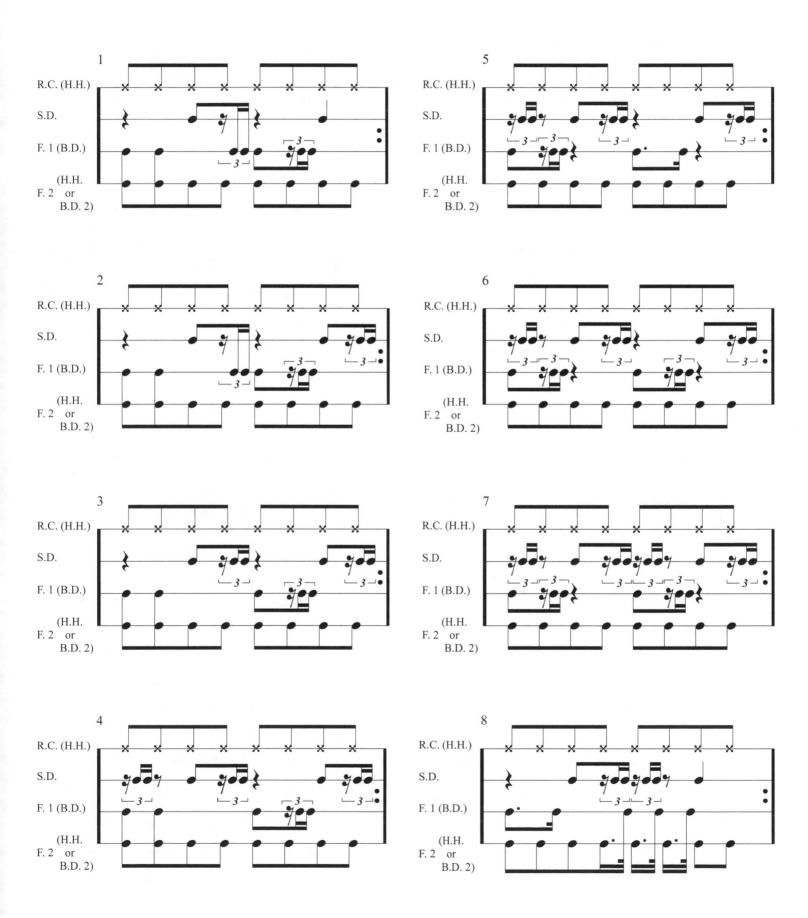

24

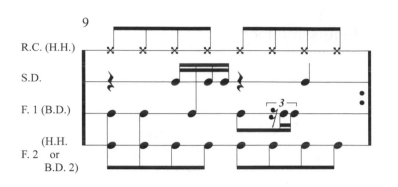

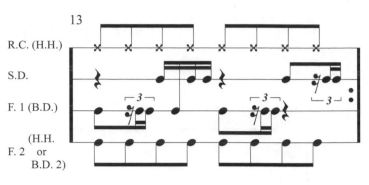

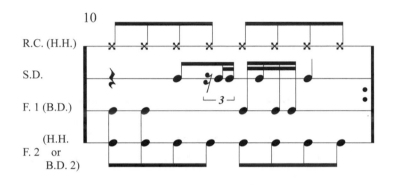

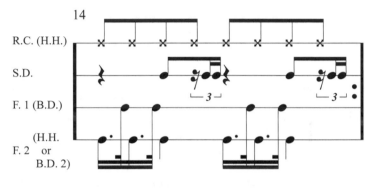

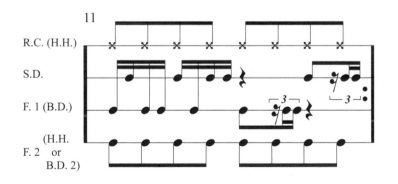

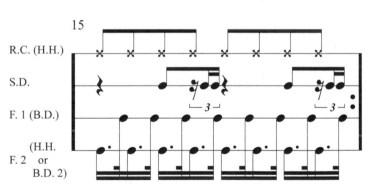

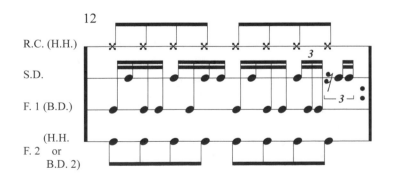

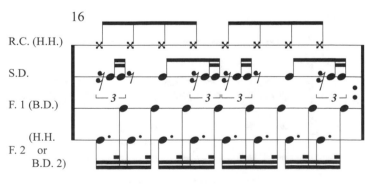

# Solo Study

# PART 8

## More sixteenth triplets

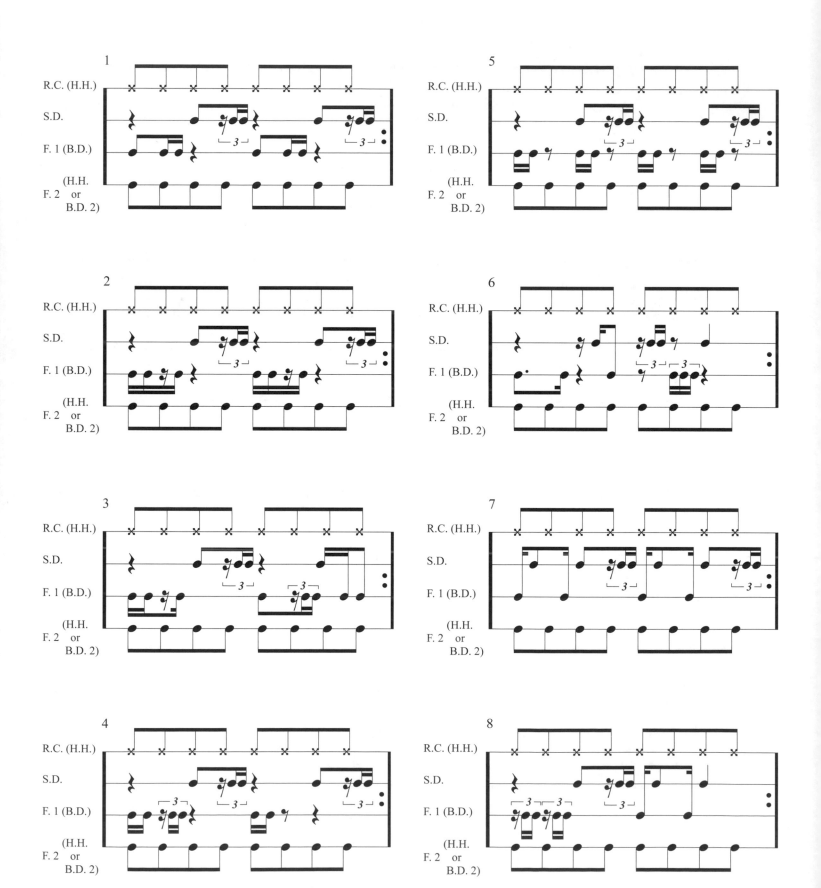

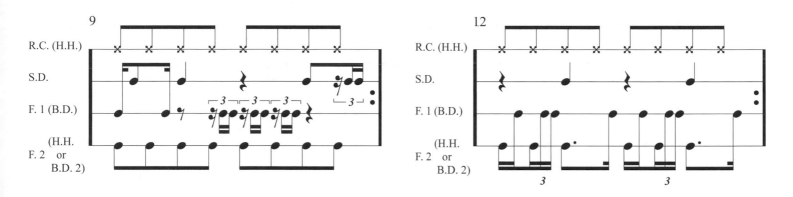

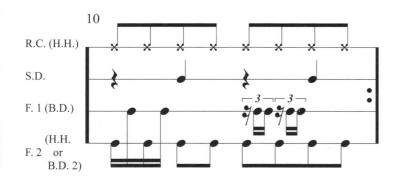

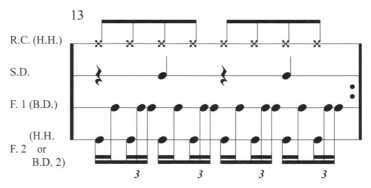

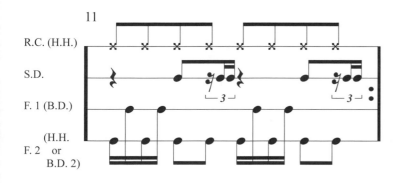

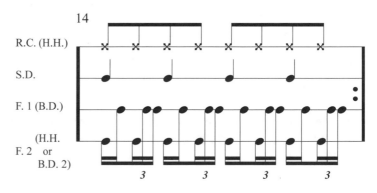

# Solo Study

R.C. (H.H.)
S.D.
F. 1 (B.D.)
(H.H.
F. 2   or
B.D. 2)

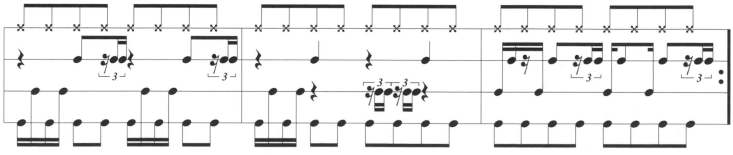

# PART 9

### Shuffle rhythms with quarter notes on the ride cymbal (H.H.)

This section has a completely different feel than the sections you've completed. The dotted eighth and sixteenth patterns should be played with a triplet feel.

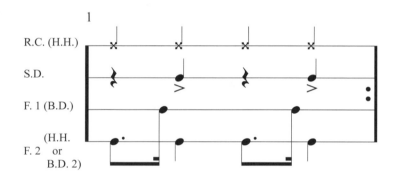

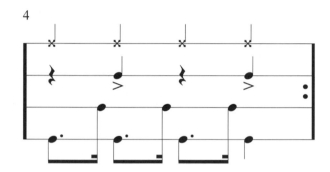

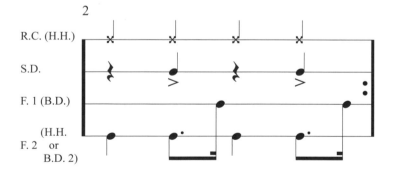

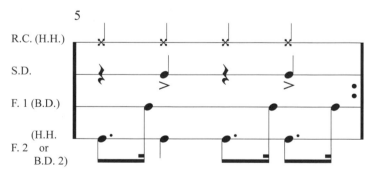

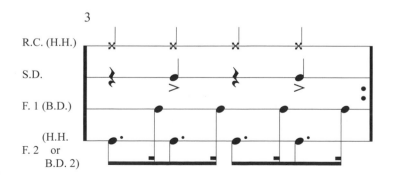

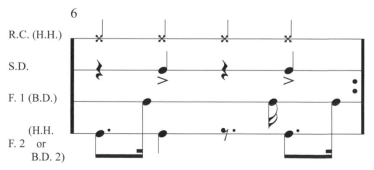

7

R.C. (H.H.)

S.D.

F. 1 (B.D.)

(H.H.
F. 2   or
B.D. 2)

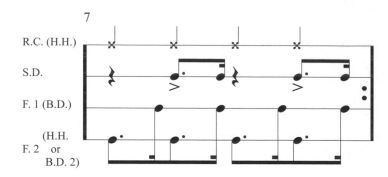

11

R.C. (H.H.)

S.D.

F. 1 (B.D.)

(H.H.
F. 2   or
B.D. 2)

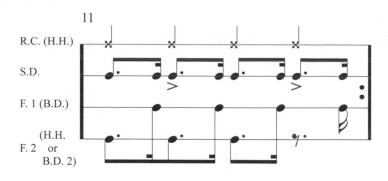

8

R.C. (H.H.)

S.D.

F. 1 (B.D.)

(H.H.
F. 2   or
B.D. 2)

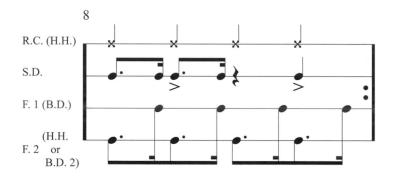

12

R.C. (H.H.)

S.D.

F. 1 (B.D.)

(H.H.
F. 2   or
B.D. 2)

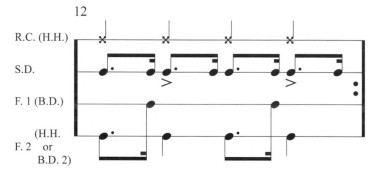

9

R.C. (H.H.)

S.D.

F. 1 (B.D.)

(H.H.
F. 2   or
B.D. 2)

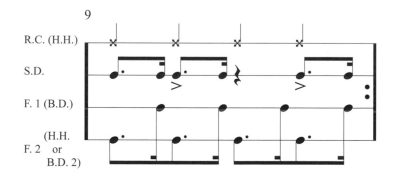

13

R.C. (H.H.)

S.D.

F. 1 (B.D.)

(H.H.
F. 2   or
B.D. 2)

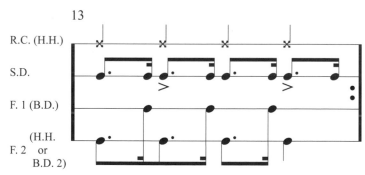

10

R.C. (H.H.)

S.D.

F. 1 (B.D.)

(H.H.
F. 2   or
B.D. 2)

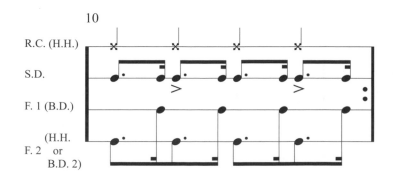

14

R.C. (H.H.)

S.D.

F. 1 (B.D.)

(H.H.
F. 2   or
B.D. 2)

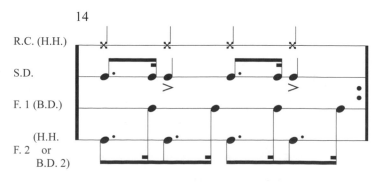

# Solo Study

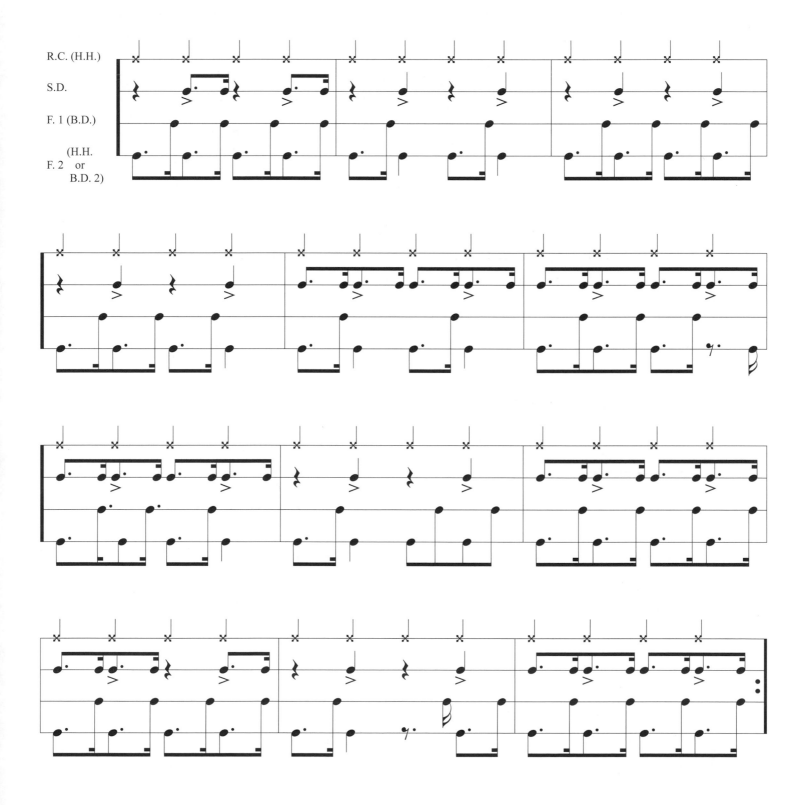

# PART 10

### Shuffle rhythms with ♪. ♪ and variations on cymbal (H.H.)

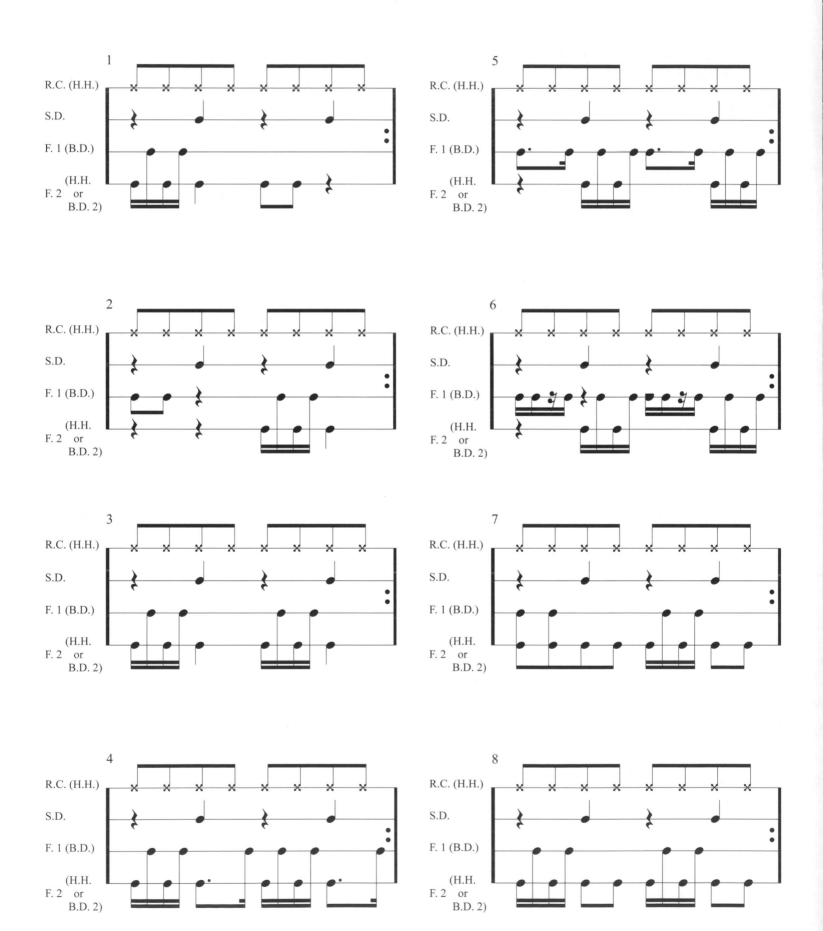

9

R.C. (H.H.)

S.D.

F. 1 (B.D.)

(H.H.
F. 2   or
B.D. 2)

10

R.C. (H.H.)

S.D.

F. 1 (B.D.)

(H.H.
F. 2   or
B.D. 2)

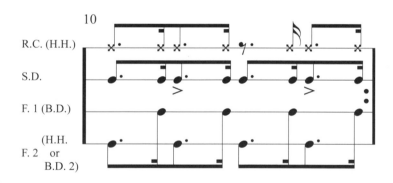

11

R.C. (H.H.)

S.D.

F. 1 (B.D.)

(H.H.
F. 2   or
B.D. 2)

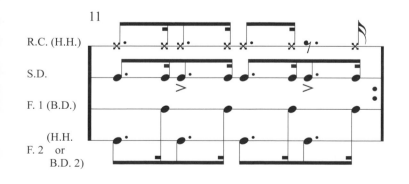

12

R.C. (H.H.)

S.D.

F. 1 (B.D.)

(H.H.
F. 2   or
B.D. 2)

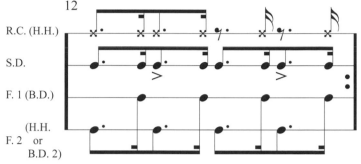

13

R.C. (H.H.)

S.D.

F. 1 (B.D.)

(H.H.
F. 2   or
B.D. 2)

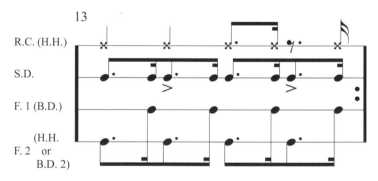

14

R.C. (H.H.)

S.D.

F. 1 (B.D.)

(H.H.
F. 2   or
B.D. 2)

# Solo Study

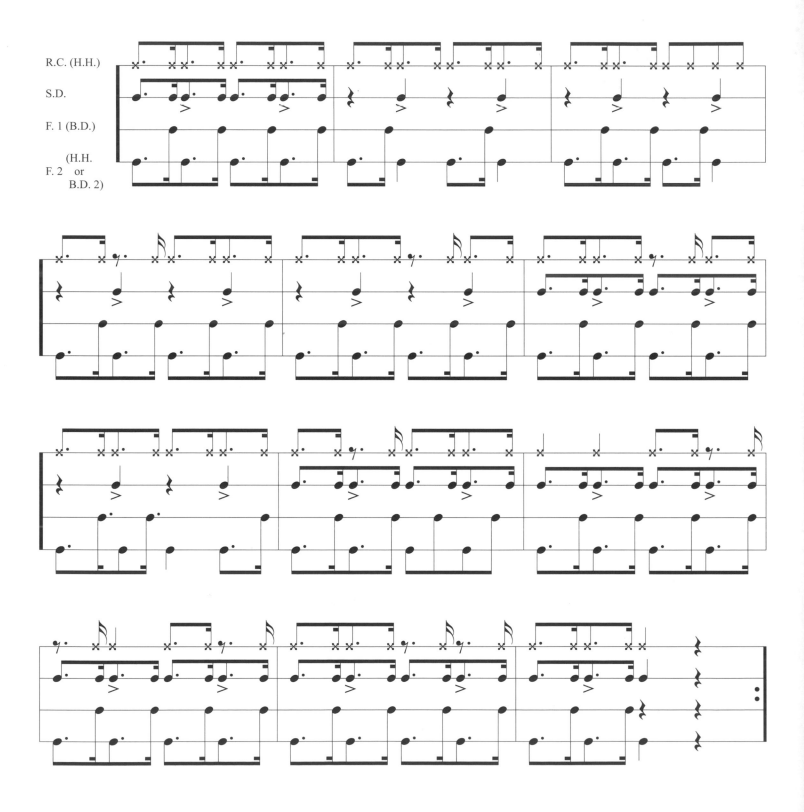

# PART 11

## 3/4 Time

The patterns you have learned work equally as well in 3/4 time. All the note relationships remain the same but there are three beats to the measure instead of four.

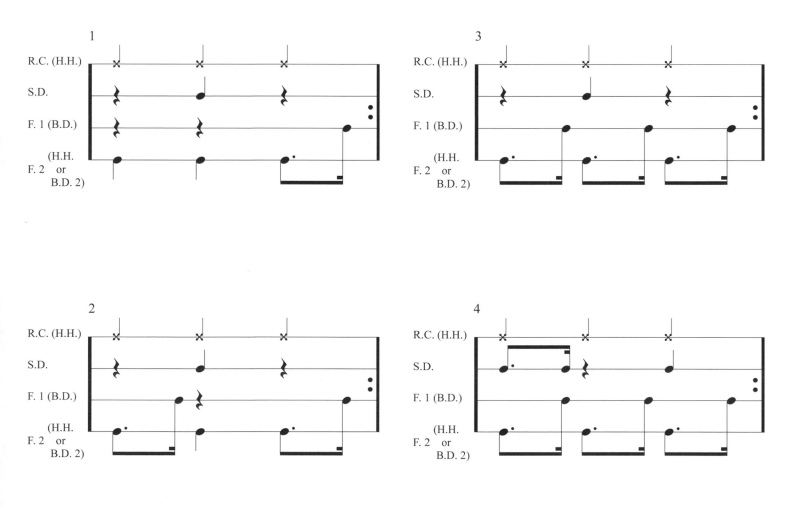

36

**5**

R.C. (H.H.)
S.D.
F. 1 (B.D.)
(H.H.
F. 2  or
B.D. 2)

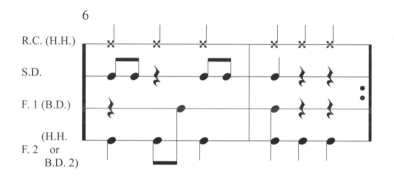

**9**

R.C. (H.H.)
S.D.
F. 1 (B.D.)
(H.H.
F. 2  or
B.D. 2)

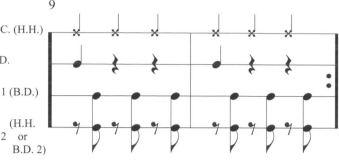

**6**

R.C. (H.H.)
S.D.
F. 1 (B.D.)
(H.H.
F. 2  or
B.D. 2)

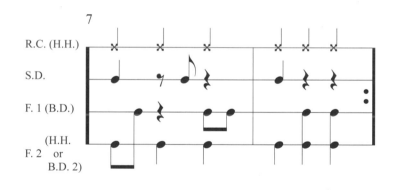

**10**

R.C. (H.H.)
S.D.
F. 1 (B.D.)
(H.H.
F. 2  or
B.D. 2)

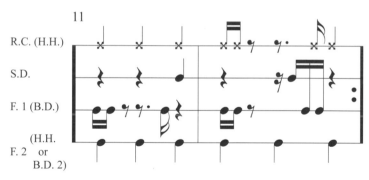

**7**

R.C. (H.H.)
S.D.
F. 1 (B.D.)
(H.H.
F. 2  or
B.D. 2)

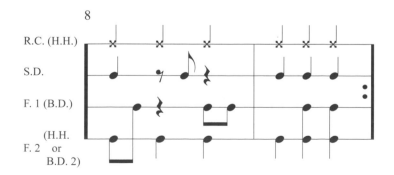

**11**

R.C. (H.H.)
S.D.
F. 1 (B.D.)
(H.H.
F. 2  or
B.D. 2)

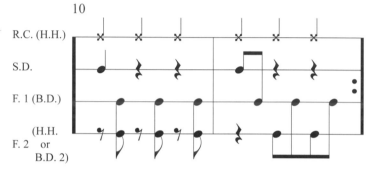

**8**

R.C. (H.H.)
S.D.
F. 1 (B.D.)
(H.H.
F. 2  or
B.D. 2)

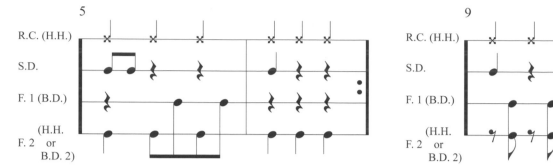

**12**

R.C. (H.H.)
S.D.
F. 1 (B.D.)
(H.H.
F. 2  or
B.D. 2)

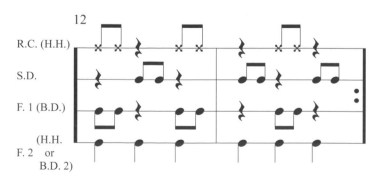

# Solo Study

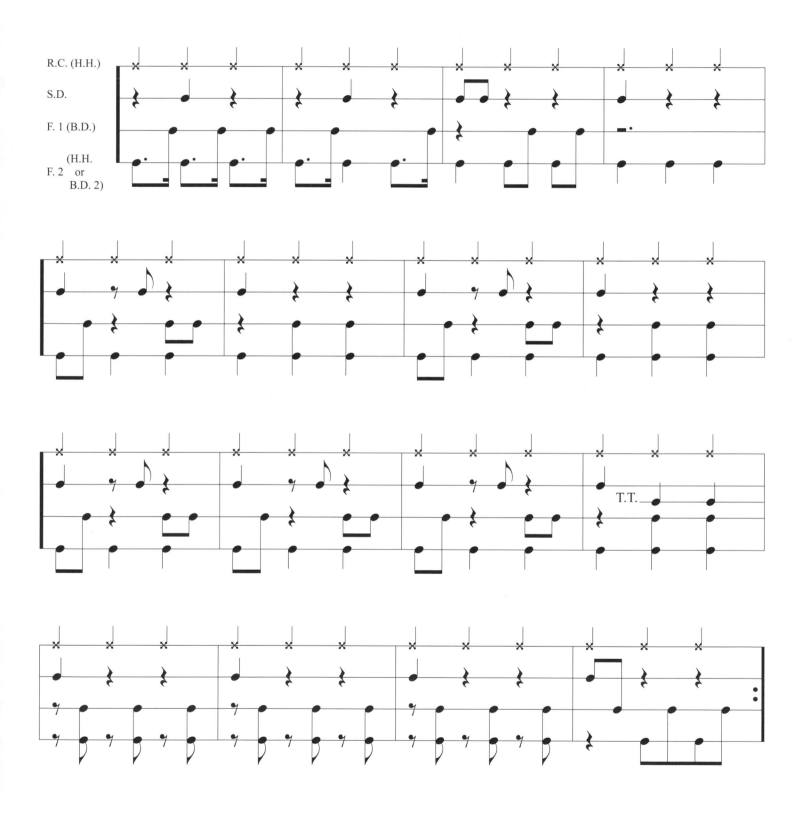

# PART 11

This section contains one and two bar fills (breaks). On these fills, the top line is written for tom tom. You will notice that it goes back to R.C. (H.H.) for the time patterns.

## Rock Fills in 4/4

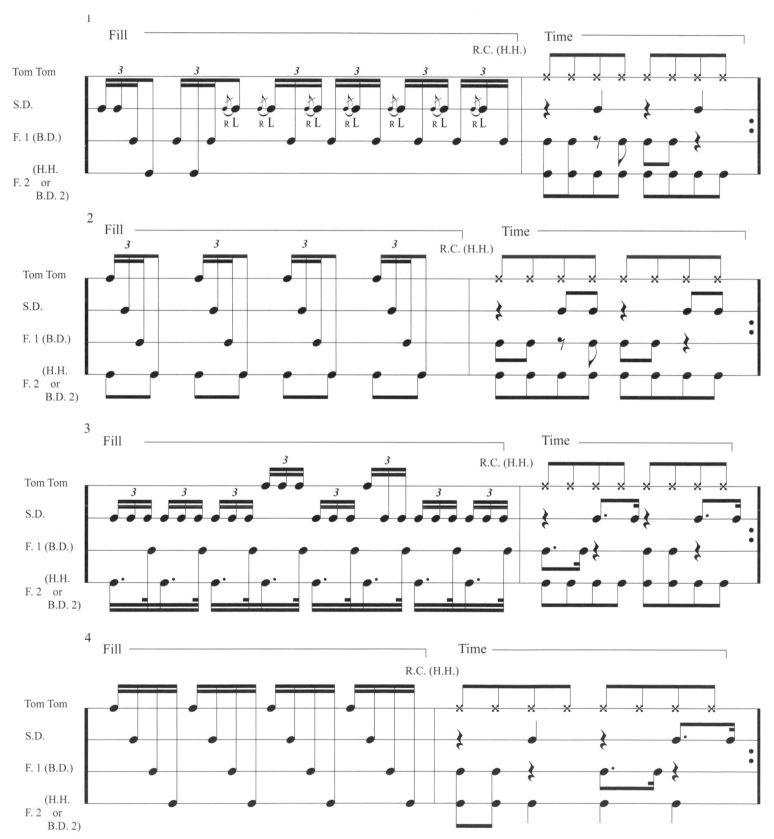

# Solo Study

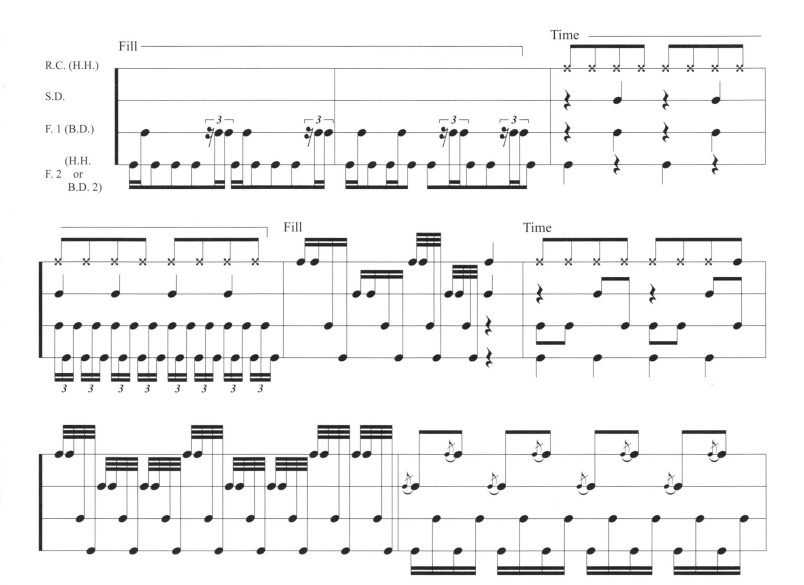

# Rock Fills in 3/4